Revised Edition

KNOWLEDGE WHIZZ 1

Kunal Savarkar Seema Chari

Collins

KNOWLEDGE WHIZZ 1

Revised Edition

Kunal Savarkar • Seema Chari

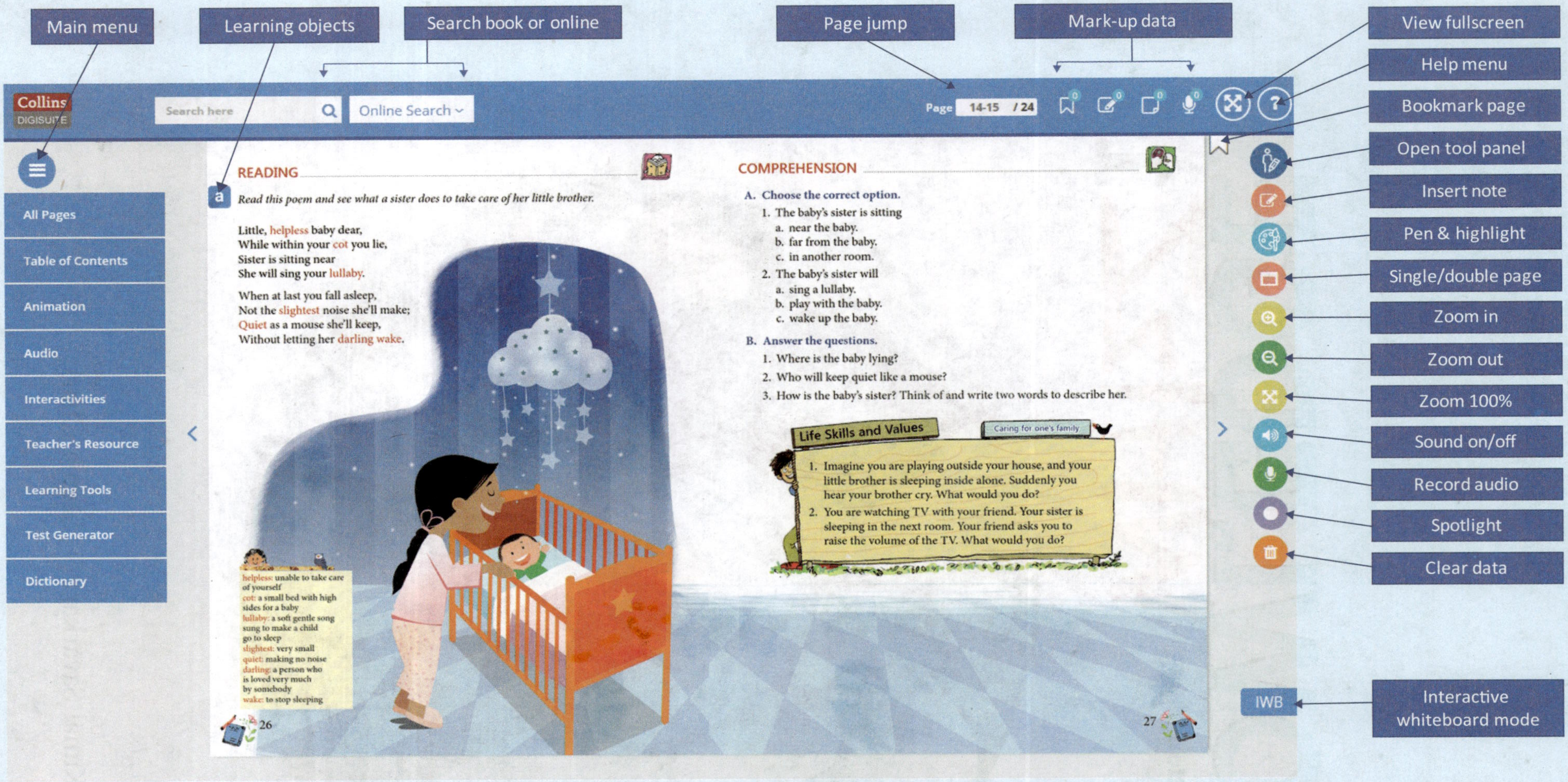

Student + Teacher			Teacher-only	
a animations	**ia** activities	**g** games	**lp** lesson plans	**tn** teacher's notes
ilt instructor-led tutorials	**w** worksheets	**v** videos	**w** worksheets	**ak** answer keys
	audio			

Preface

Welcome to ***Knowledge Whizz*** Version 2.0! Our belief that knowledge is for everyone has resonated well across the country, with thousands of school children now using the series, thereby reinforcing our conviction that general knowledge is not the exclusive preserve of a few quizzers. In this multimedia age, knowledge is everywhere, but sourcing, assimilating and recalling it is a skill that can be learned!

Knowledge Whizz, now in its second edition, is a unique series that aims to offer general knowledge covering a wide range of subjects, both curricular as well as extra-curricular, to children from six to thirteen years of age. These are GK books for learning, not quiz books for testing.

Salient features of the series

- Each task comprises at least two kinds of inputs to help children arrive at the answers and acquire knowledge at the same time.
- Tasks cover a wide range of topics presented with a twist. For instance, history includes the story of the automobile, bicycle, cinema, cricket and flight; science includes accidental inventions and discoveries; geography comes alive through associative information and culturally rich chapters. Language and literature cover trivia and etymology, two wonderful learning tools.
- Themes from modern life such as gaming, media, business and finance are extensively explored as well as tidbits about the quirky and the quotidian.
- India-specific content presented beautifully through fun, richly illustrated tasks, designed to whet the curiosity of children and inspire them to explore their beautiful country in all its diversity. New chapters on North East India bring the vibrancy and uniqueness of this relatively lesser known part of India to children everywhere.
- The books do not expect children to be pre-equipped with knowledge but instead reward inquisitiveness by giving them workoutable tasks.
- The artistic and colourful layouts make the presentation more accessible, exciting and alluring whilst facilitating self-learning.
- Special features are an exciting mixed bag of environment education, life skills, values, quick quizzes, cool facts, cool activity, evaluation of multiple intelligences and Higher Order Thinking Skills to make children become well-rounded individuals.
- Brand new features incorporated into Version 2.0 include Aptitudes, aiming to hone and cement specific verbal, visual and logical aptitudes through the common lens of general knowledge, Safety Science, which draws our attention tn the science behind the measures we should take to stay safe wherever we are, and Game, to bring a good dose of fun into learning.

We gratefully acknowledge the contribution of the Xpress Minds Edutainment team, whose inputs have been invaluable for this second edition.

We are certain that this series will open up the world of general knowledge and make learning a fun, instinctive and rewarding process for all.

~ Kunal Savarkar and Seema Chari

In This Book ...

Multiple Intelligence tasks focus on the 8 Intelligences: interpersonal, intrapersonal, bodily kinesthetic, visual-spatial, logical reasoning, verbal-linguistic, naturalistic and musical. Each page explores 3-4 intelligences to encourage learners to learn in their own way and is not to be used for assessment.

Higher Order Thinking Skills (HOTS) pages encourage critical thinking and teach learners to analyse and evaluate information. Cool quizmaster, Kunal Savarkar, helps students become knowledge detectives and skilled quizzers.

Are You a Knowledge Whizz?

Learn how to become a top quizzer.

Have you seen questions that ask you to find out the odd one? They are very easy to answer if you follow some steps.

Cool Activity
Fun activities to learn through doing.

Cool Quiz
Encourages research to find solutions.

Current Affairs
Visit **www.collins.in/knowledgewhizz** for Current Affairs updates and weekly quizzes.

Tidy Up!

A. *Look at the untidy room. Clean the room by joining things to their proper places in the second picture.*

Values pages focus on inculcating values, morals, ethics and right attitudes in students through to-do tasks.

Life Skills pages expose learners to problems in real-life situations to help them learn to take decisions.

What Can You Do by Yourself?

Aptitude

Aptitude Tasks are designed to teach children to develop specific skills such as sequencing, classification, analogies, etc., through rebuses, matching, sorting and pattern activities, with step-by-step tips on how to solve them.

COOL FACT

Did you know that the stars that you see in the sky are actually circles?

Green Earth

Green Earth page focuses on environmental issues and imbibes the right attitude towards conservation of environment.

COOL FACT

Factoids linked to the content of the page. The fun element in them will make you say, 'Hey! Cool to know that.'

Safety Science

Safety is not just a notion; it is a science, which means it is guided by research, facts and figures. From home to school, public places to controlled environments, we can do a lot to keep ourselves safe. The Safety Science chapters in each book show us how."

Game

Life is a game! Each book in the series has at least one puzzle, maze or strategy-based activity, always with a GK twist, but with the added fell-good incentive of "winning the game".

Quiz Yourself are quick quizzes to assess what the children have learned in the book. The main themes and the cool facts will all form the basis of the Quiz Yourself section, intended as a self-evaluation tool from books 3 to 8.

Detailed Contents

Contents

My Family Tree

Draw or paste the pictures of your father's parents and your mother's parents. Also paste the pictures of your parents, your brothers and sisters, pets (if you have any) and, of course, your own picture.

Now, write the names of everyone in your family.

Take Care

Do you keep yourself clean?

In the pictures below, draw a smiley ☺ for the clean child and a sad face ☹ for the child who is careless about being clean.

1.

2.

3.

4.

5.

6.

7.

8.

9.

10.

11.

12.

13.

14.

1

The Shape Clown

Look at the clown. He is juggling different shapes. Can you complete their names? Look at the shapes on the clown's dress and see how many you can count.

1. _ _ R _ L _
2. _ _ IA _ _ _ LE
3. _ Q _ _ _ E
4. _ _ C _ AN _ _ E
5. _ _ A _
6. _ T A _

star
circle
oval
triangle
rectangle
square

COOL FACT

Did you know that the stars you see in the sky are actually circles? They are so far away that they twinkle and look like pointed stars!

NATURAL WORLD

2

Mother and Babies

Join the dots and trace the path from each mother animal to her baby. Say the names of the mother and complete the names of the babies too.

COOL FACT

Many big animals such as whale, elephant, camel, giraffe, hippo, rhino, yak, reindeer (and many more) have babies called calves. A chunk of iceberg that breaks off is also called a calf!

LANGUAGE AND LITERATURE

3

Rhymes We Sing

These nursery rhymes have some words missing. Look at the picture clues given on both the pages and fill in the blanks with the right letters. One has been done for you.

Baa baa black 1. __j__

Have you any 2. ______?

Yes sir, yes sir, three 3. ______ full.

One for my master, one for my dame,

And one for the little 4. ______ who lives down the lane.

a.

b.

c.

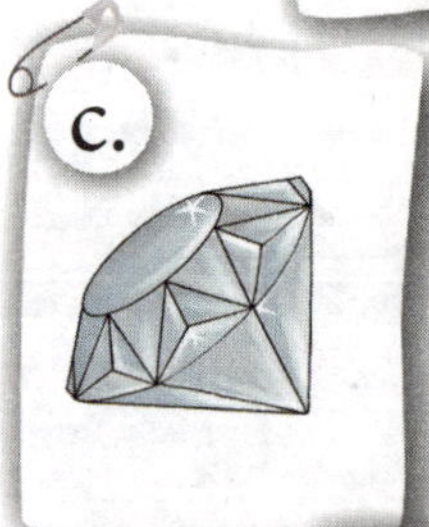

d.

Hickory dickory dock,

The 5. ______ ran up the clock;

The 6. ______ struck 7. ______,

The 8. ______ ran down,

Hickory dickory dock.

e.

COOL FACT Did you know that the rhymes you recite today are more than three hundred years old?

Mary had a little 9. ______, little 10. ______,

little 11. ______,

Mary had a little 12. ______,

Whose fleece was white as 13. ______.

And everywhere that Mary went, Mary went, Mary went,

And everywhere that Mary went, the 14. ______ was sure to go.

f.

g.

h.

i.

j.

k.

l.

m.

Twinkle, twinkle, little 15. ______,

How I wonder what you are.

Up above the 16. ______ so high,

Like a 17. ______ in the 18. ______.

What Can You Do by Yourself?

Read the actions. Put a tick (✓) for actions you can do yourself. Cross (×) for actions you need help to do.

1. Using things made of glass ☐
2. Cutting with a knife ☐
3. Bathing ☐
4. Wearing clothes ☐
5. Tidying your toys and books ☐
6. Using mobile phones ☐
7. Taking medicines ☐
8. Tying shoelaces ☐
9. Cutting with child scissors ☐
10. Packing your school bag ☐

Fruits Inside Out!

If you cut some fruits, you will see that the colour inside the fruit is different from the colour of its skin.

A. Colour the skins and the insides of the fruits given.

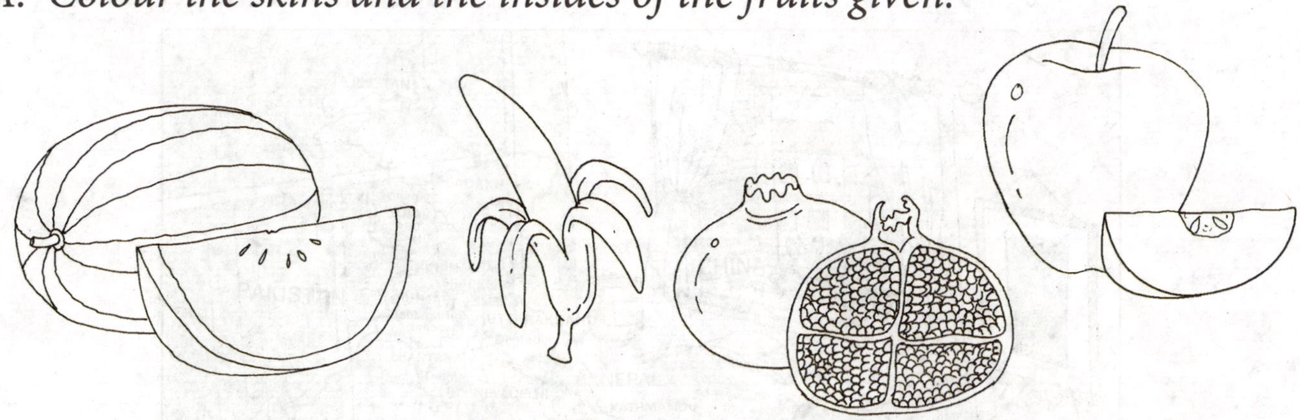

B. Look at the basket of fruits. Count and write in the circles how many of each fruit you can see.

COOL FACT The world's biggest and heaviest fruit growing on a tree is the jackfruit. Its name comes from the Portuguese word *jaca*, which itself comes from the Malayalam word *chakka*.

Tidy Up!

A. *Look at the untidy room in the first picture. Clean the room by joining things to their proper places in the second picture. One has been done for you.*

1\.

2\.

B. *Now look again at the untidy room and complete the answers below.*

1. How many books do you see?

   I see ________ books.

2. How many pairs of shoes do you see?

   I see ________ pair of shoes.

3. How many toys do you see scattered on the floor?

   I see ________ toys.

4. How many pencils do you see on the table?

   I see ________ pencils.

C. *Look at this picture. Some children are not behaving very well in the park. Find the wrong actions and draw a circle around them.*

5 Pet Food

Look at the given pictures. There are rows of food for each animal. Tick (✓) the foods that the animal normally eats.

COOL FACT The dog is called a man's best friend. But actually, there are more pet cats than pet dogs in the world.

ENTERTAINMENT

6

Cute Cartoons

Read the rhymes, see the pictures and write the names of these famous cartoons.

Thomas the Tank Engine	Pikachu	Teletubbies
Spongebob Squarepants	Doraemon	

1. 

Two big teeth, a red tie,
Wearing square pants, who am I?

____

2. 

Nobita Nobi is my friend, you know,
I'm a blue cat, who's a robot!

____

3. 

I am a Pokemon with black-tip ears,
Yellow and chubby, my dears!

____

4. 

Tinky-winky, Laa Laa, Dipsy and Po,
With a baby-face sun, off we go!

____

5. 

A little blue engine with a happy face,
I chug along all over the place!

____

Cool Quiz

I have a white tummy and a black coat, I'm a cute little bird who's a great sport! Who am I? ______________

AROUND THE WORLD

7

Seasons Check

A. *Look at the pictures of the three main seasons, summer, rainy and winter. Colour the circles green for things that match the season in the pictures and red if they do not.*

B. *Draw a picture of your favourite season.*

COOL FACTS

- Mango, the king of fruits, is found in the summer season.
- December and January are the coldest months in India.

SPORTS

8

Summer or Winter Sports

The sports given below are played either during summer or winter season. Look at the pictures and write S for Summer sports and W for Winter sports in the boxes.

1.

badminton ☐

2.

skiing ☐

3.

ice hockey ☐

4.

tennis ☐

5.

swimming

6.

bobsleigh

7.

toboggan

8.

football

9.

luge

10.

field hockey

SCIENCE

9 Alive or Not

All the things around us can be either living or non-living.

A. *Colour the squares next to living things green and non-living things red.*

1. 

2. 

3. 

4. 

5. 

6. 

7. 

8. 

9. 

10. 

B. *Now draw two each of your favourite living and non-living things.*

living

non-living

living

non-living

COOL FACT

How will you find out if a thing has life or not? Ask yourself these three questions and you will know.

- Does it need food and water?
- Does it need air or water to breathe?
- Does it grow?

If the answer to all these questions is a 'Yes', then the thing has life.

Tell a Tale

The pictures below tell a story, but they are all mixed up. Put numbers 1, 2, 3, 4, 5, 6, 7 and 8 next to the pictures and tell the story in the right order.

a.

b.

c.

Moral: Unity is strength. This means if we are together, we will always be strong.

ART

10 Colour Splash

Recite the poem and have fun with colours!

Colours

— by Christina Rossetti

What is pink? A rose is pink,
By a fountain's brink.

What is red? A poppy's red,
In its barley bed.

What is blue? The sky is blue,
Where the clouds float thro'.

What else is pink?
Colour only the pink things!

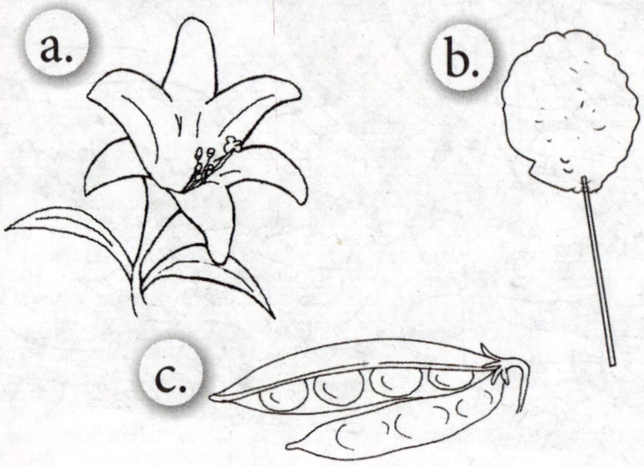

a. b. c.

What else is red?
Colour only the red things!

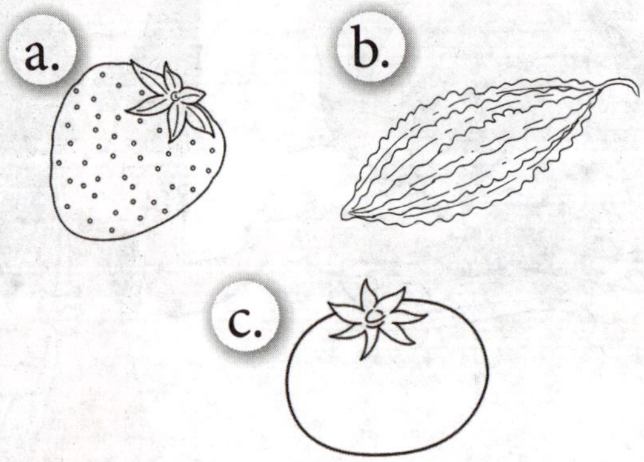

a. b. c.

What else is blue?
Colour only the blue things!

a. b. c.

COOL FACT There are seven colours in the rainbow. Seen in order these are violet, indigo, blue, green, yellow, orange and red.

What else is white?
Colour the thing that is not white!

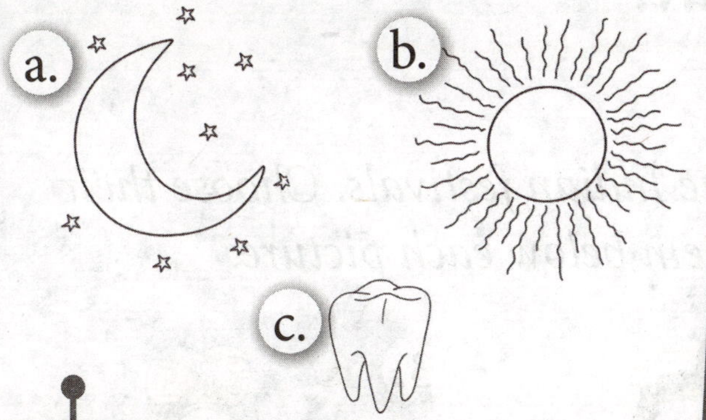

What else is yellow?
Colour only the yellow things!

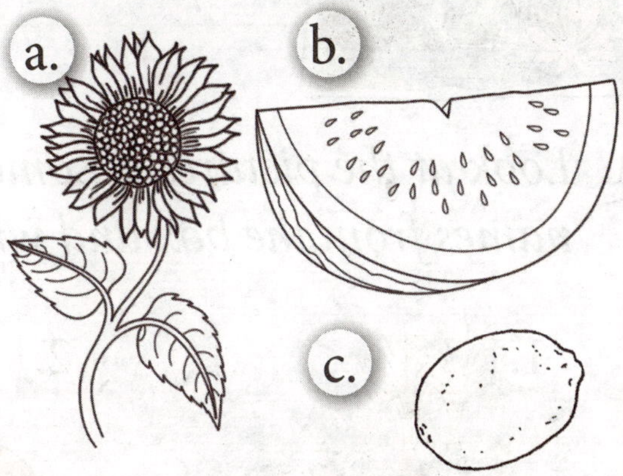

What is white? A swan is white,
Sailing in the light.

What is yellow? Pears are yellow,
Rich and ripe and mellow.

What is green? The grass is green,
With small flowers between.

What is violet? Clouds are violet,
In the summer twilight.

What is orange? Why, an orange,
Just an orange!

What else is green?
Colour only the green things!

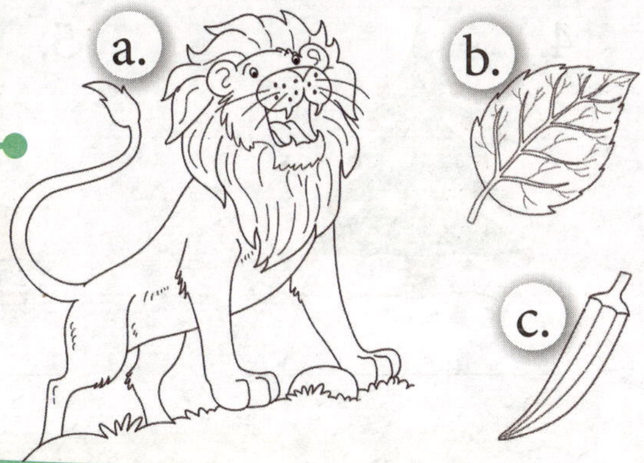

What else is orange?
Colour only the orange things!

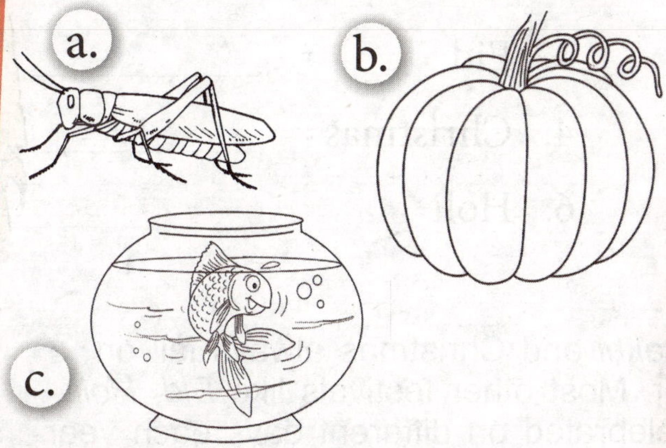

What else is violet?
Colour only the violet things!

11

Festival Fun!

A. *Look at the pictures of some of the Indian festivals. Choose their names from the box and write them below each picture.*

1. 
____

2. 
____

3. 
____

4. 
____

5. 
____

6. 
____

Buddha Purnima	Diwali	Christmas
Janmashtami	Eid	Holi

B. *On what dates, will these festivals be celebrated this year? Find out the dates and write them here.*

1. Diwali ________ 2. Eid ________
3. Janmashtami ________ 4. Christmas ________
5. Buddha Purnima ________ 6. Holi ________

COOL FACT Festivals like *Lohri*, *Baisakhi* and Christmas always fall on the same day every year. Most other festivals like *Eid*, *Holi*, Easter and *Diwali* are celebrated on different days each year.

INDIA

12

My India

Look at the map. India has 28 states. Some of the states touch the sea.

Colour only the states that touch the sea and say how many there are. Try to learn their names!

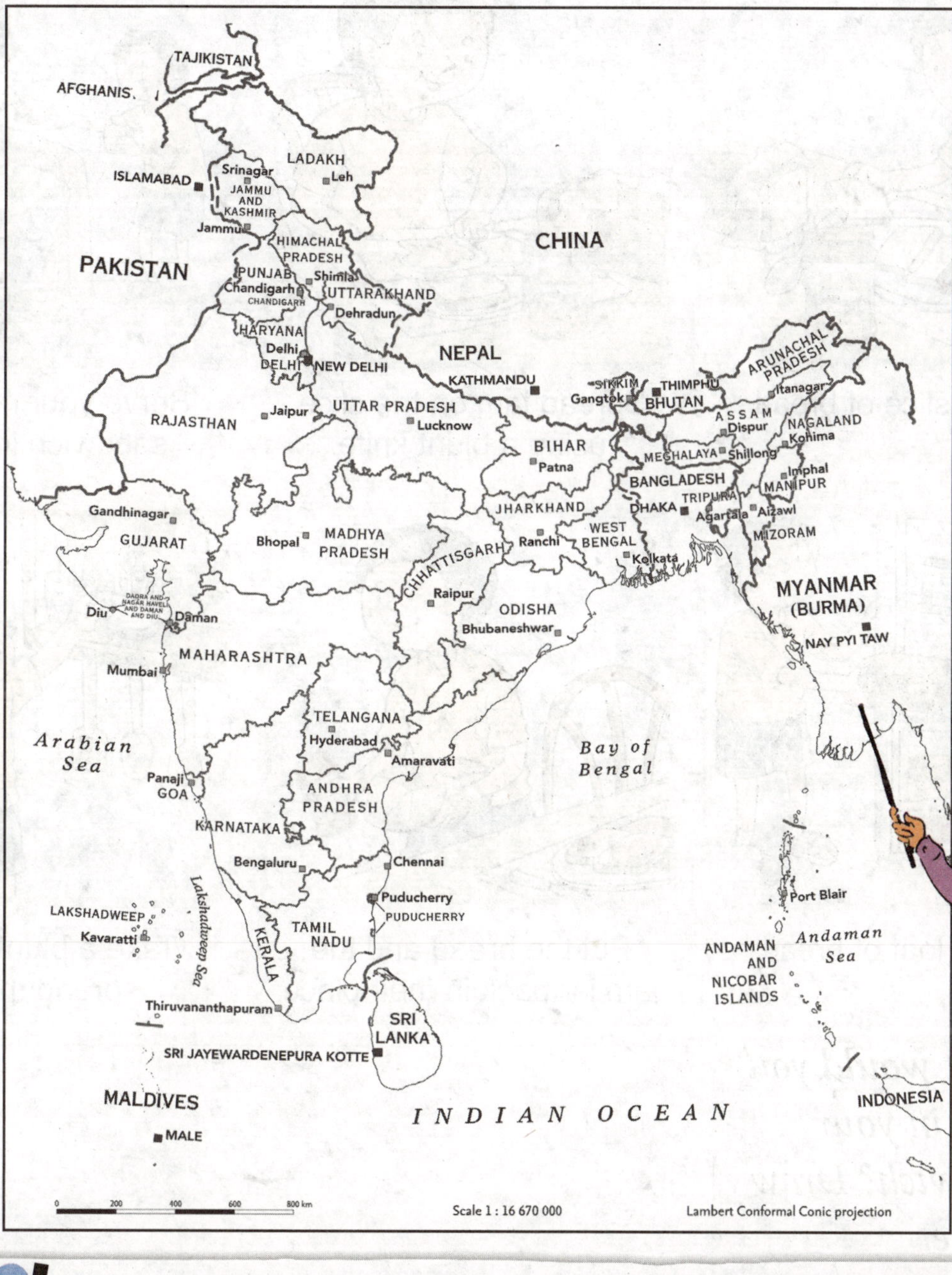

COOL FACT The Andaman and Nicobar Islands and the Lakshadweep Islands are also a part of India. These are union territories and not states.

Mummy, Are You Hungry?

A. *Make a sandwich for Mummy and you! Write 1, 2, 3, 4, 5 and 6 in the boxes to put the pictures in the right order.*

a.

Take a slice of bread

b.

Spread jam on the slice using a blunt knife

c.

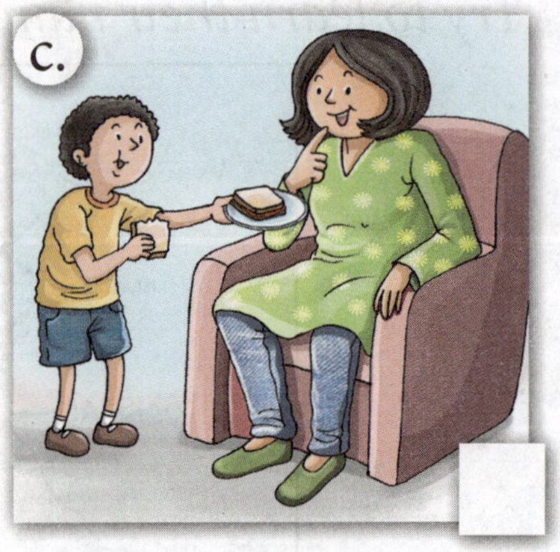

Serve your mother the sandwich in a plate

d.

Take a loaf of bread

e.

Put the bread and the jam jar back in their place

f.

Take a blunt knife to spread the jam

B. *What would you want in your sandwich? Draw it here.*

SCIENCE

13 Tasty Foods

Foods can be sweet, sour, salty, bitter or spicy.

In the taste chart, each row has foods of the given taste except one food. Circle the one odd food in each row.

1. SWEET

cake | ice cream | mango | chips | honey

2. SOUR

tamarind | raw mango | mango pickle | lemon | milk

3. SALTY

pizza | paratha | soup | chocolate | chips

4. BITTER

bittergourd | neem | medicine | cupcake | coffee

5. SPICY

black pepper | candy | chilli powder | ginger | green chilly

COOL FACT You taste using your nose and tongue together. So, when you have a cold, you can hardly taste anything!

Save, Don't Waste

Water, light and clean air are precious. We must not waste them. We should use plastic, paper, oil and petrol as less as possible.

A. *Read these actions and look at the pictures. Which actions help you save or waste? In the boxes, draw a smiley ☺ if you save and a sad face ☹ if you waste.*

1.

Keep the TV on all day

2.

Use cloth bags to do shopping

3.

Switch off all lights when not in use

4.

Keep the tap water running while brushing teeth

5.

Go to school in your own car (and not the school bus)

6.

Wrap a birthday gift in newspaper

7.

Spend 1 hour in the shower

8.

Sleep with all the lights on

9.

Use a lift instead of the stairs

10.

Leave the tap dripping after use

B. *Now turn the page and play the Caring Game!*

The Caring Game

Do you save or do you waste? Play this game and find out!

The game begins from START and ends at FINISH. Move the same number of steps as the number on the dice you throw. Follow what is written on the picture square. The first person (or team) to reach FINISH is the winner!

You will need 1 set of dice and 6 counters. You can make your dice by writing numbers from 1 to 6 on the sides of an eraser and use sharpeners as counters to play this game.

14 Sportsworthy

Look at the pictures of certain things needed to play sports. Write two things required to play the sports listed below. One has been done for you.

1. Football = k + i
2. Badminton = ______ + ______
3. Table Tennis = ______ + ______
4. Tennis = ______ + ______
5. Cricket = ______ + ______
6. Basketball = ______ + ______

COOL FACT

A shuttlecock is also called a 'birdie' and normally has sixteen feathers.

ENTERTAINMENT

15

Panchatantra Animals

The *Panchatantra* is a collection of stories for children. There are many animals in each story and a moral at the end of the story.

A. *Look at the animals from three Panchatantra stories. The pictures of the animals are mixed up. Join the animals to the name of each story.*

1.

2.

3.

Titles

a. The Crows and the Owls

b. The Monkey and the Crocodile

c. The Lion and the Rabbit

i.

ii.

iii.

B. *Now tell the story that you like best!*

16

Animal Farm

Do you know how animals call? Fill in the blanks in the song with the call of the animal. You may use the help box. Now sing the song!

Old McDonald had a farm, E-I-E-I-O!
And on that farm he had some **cows**
E-I-E-I-O!
With a ____-____ here,
and a ____-____ there,
Here a ____, there a ____,
everywhere a ____-____.

Old McDonald had a farm, E-I-E-I-O!
And on that farm he had some **sheep**
E-I-E-I-O!
With a ____-____ here,
and a ____-____ there,
Here a ____, there a ____,
everywhere a ____-____.

Old McDonald had a farm, E-I-E-I-O!
And on that farm he had some **horses**
E-I-E-I-O!
With a ____-____ here,
and a ____-____ there,
Here a ____, there a ____,
everywhere a ____-____.

Old McDonald had a farm, E-I-E-I-O!
And on that farm he had some **ducks**
E-I-E-I-O!
With a ____-____ here,
and a ____-____ there,
Here a ____, there a ____,
everywhere a ____-____.

Old McDonald had a farm, E-I-E-I-O!
And on that farm he had some **hens**
E-I-E-I-O!
With a ____-____ here,
and a ____-____ there,
Here a ____, there a ____,
everywhere a ____-____.

Old McDonald had a farm, E-I-E-I-O!
And on that farm he had some **dogs**
E-I-E-I-O!
With a ____-____ here,
and a ____-____ there,
Here a ____, there a ____,
everywhere a ____-____.

Old McDonald had a farm, E-I-E-I-O!
And on that farm he had some **cats**
E-I-E-I-O!
With a ____-____ here,
and a ____-____ there,
Here a ____, there a ____,
everywhere a ____-____.

quack-quack
moo-moo
bow-wow
meow-meow
baa-baa
neigh-neigh
cluck-cluck

COOL FACT
Children all over the world sing this song in Arabic, French, German, Italian and many other languages.

Home Sweet Home

Match the animals with their homes.

1.

cow

a.

stable

2.

dog

b.

pen

3.

hen

c.

kennel

4.

horse

d.

coop

5.

sheep

e.

shed

MI

Underwater Fun

Look at the two pictures. In the first picture, we can see things under the sea. In the second one, some of those things are missing. Circle the things in the first picture that are missing in the second picture.

1\.

2\.

COOL FACT

Did you know that most of the earth is covered with oceans and seas? This is why our planet looks blue when we see it from outer space.

LANGUAGE AND LITERATURE

17 Fairy Tales

A. *Look at the pictures and read the given clues. Tick (✓) the fairy tale the with which they match.*

1.

The princess lets down her hair for the prince to climb.

a. Pied Piper of Hamelin ☐

b. Rapunzel ☐

2.

The beautiful princess lived in the forest with her little friends.

a. Snow White and the Seven Dwarfs ☐

b. Cinderella ☐

3.

The little girl wore a red hood.

a. Beauty and the Beast ☐

b. Little Red Riding Hood ☐

4.

The two children found a house made of cakes and sweets in the forest.

a. Puss in Boots ☐

b. Hansel and Gretel ☐

5.

When the puppet lied, his nose became longer.

a. Jack and the Beanstalk ☐

b. Pinocchio ☐

6.

The little girl ate the porridge and went off to sleep.

a. Goldilocks and the Three Bears ☐

b. The Frog Prince ☐

B. Who is your favourite character from a fairy tale? Write the name of the story and draw the picture of your favourite character.

My favourite fairy tale is ______________________________.

COOL FACT

Hans Christian Andersen wrote many famous fairy tales. In Copenhagen, Denmark, there is a statue of the *Little Mermaid*, one of his most loved characters. Here she is, sitting on her rock!

Are You a Knowledge Whizz?

Learn how to become a top quizzer.

Have you seen questions that ask you to find out the odd one? They are very easy to answer if you follow some steps.

A. Let us try to find the odd one in this set of names.

Follow the steps below.

1. First find what is common to all the words.
   a. We see that all of them are names.
   b. We see that all the names start with 'A'.
2. What is different in all the words?

   Ans. Ajay, Aryan and Arnav are boys' names; BUT Amya is not. It is a girl's name.

   So we know that Amya is the odd one.

B. *Now find the odd ones in the sets below.*

Example : a. mouth b. nose c. knee d. ear

Clue: All these are parts of the body. But while mouth, nose and ear are all on the face, the knee is not. So "knee" is the odd one out! Try these others.

1. a. cricket b. chess c. hockey d. football
2. a. jeans b. shoes c. slippers d. boots
3. a. pencil b. notebook c. handbag d. sharpener
4. a. bus b. bicycle c. car d. truck
5. a. sweater b. shorts c. jacket d. gloves

C. *Draw the odd ones in B in the given space.*

LOGICAL REASONING

18 

The Right Place

Everything should be kept in their proper places!

A. *Look at the pictures of things found in your home. Where do you find them? Write their names in the correct lists given on the next page.*

a. 
bed

b. 
ruler

c. 
pencil

d. 
bowl

e. 

book

f. 
bucket

g. 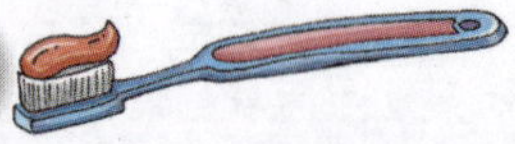
toothbrush

h. 
cupboard

i. 
crayons

j. 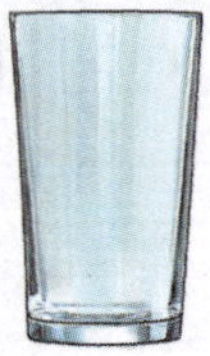
glass

k. 
bedside lamp

l. 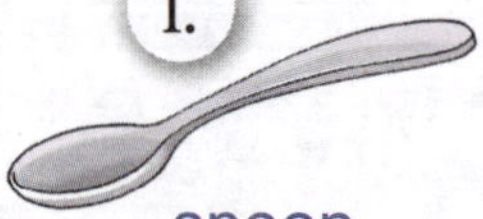
spoon

m. 

toothpaste

n. 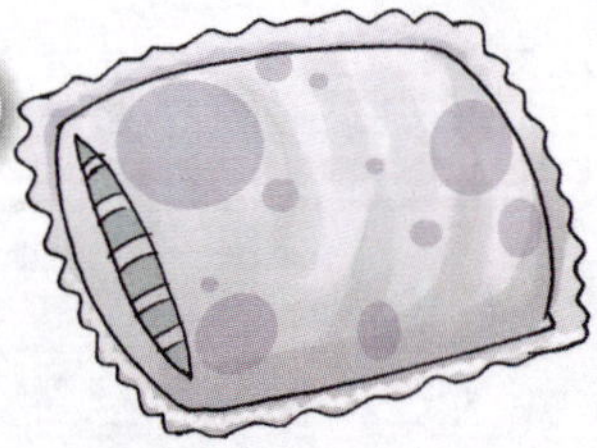
pillow

o. 
plate

p. 
soap

Bedroom	Bathroom

School bag	Dining table

B. *What do you keep in your cupboard? Write any four things.*

COOL FACT One of the largest homes in the world is the *Rashtrapati Bhavan* at New Delhi. This is where the President of India lives.

AROUND THE WORLD

19 Interesting Jobs

A. *Some people work with their hands. Match the pictures with the names.*

1.

2.

a. farmer

b. cobbler

c. baker

d. tailor

e. fisherman

f. gardener

3.

4.

5.

6.

B. *Now look at some more pictures. Have you ever seen these people at work? Ask your parents or grandparents if they knew about these jobs when they were children.*

disc jockey

cartoonist

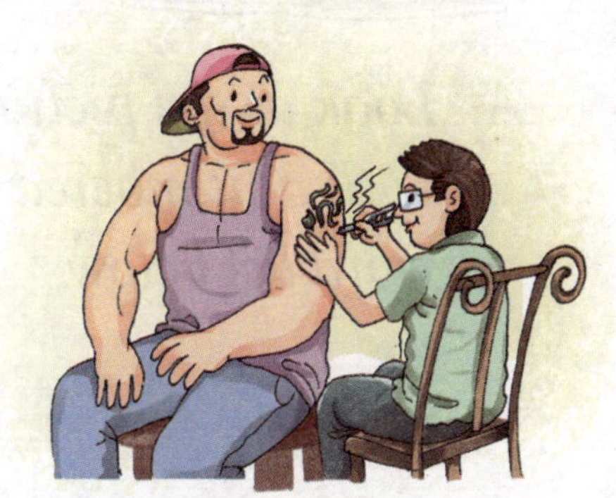

tattooist

quizmaster

rock star

choreographer

flight attendant

metro driver

Draw and say an interesting job of one of your parents or relatives

20 We Use Them Every Day

A. *Look at the picture of the playground. Some things are marked with a numbered circle. Write down the names of these things in the word list below.*

1. M ___ G
2. J ___ R
3. B ___ L ___
4. B ___ T
5. C ___ T
6. D ___ G
7. M ___ N
8. B ___ G
9. F ___ N
10. C ___ P

B. Some words in the word list sound the same as names of the things given below. Pair them by writing the correct numbers in the circles.

a.

b.

c.
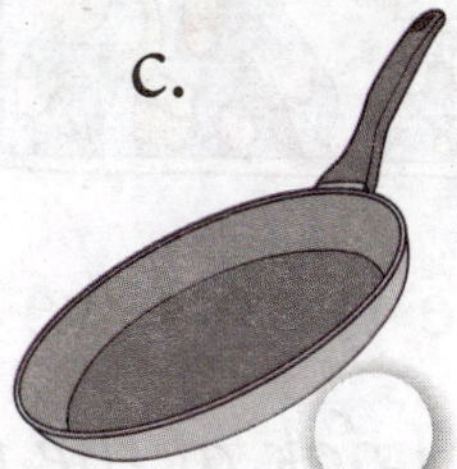

d.

e.

f.

g.
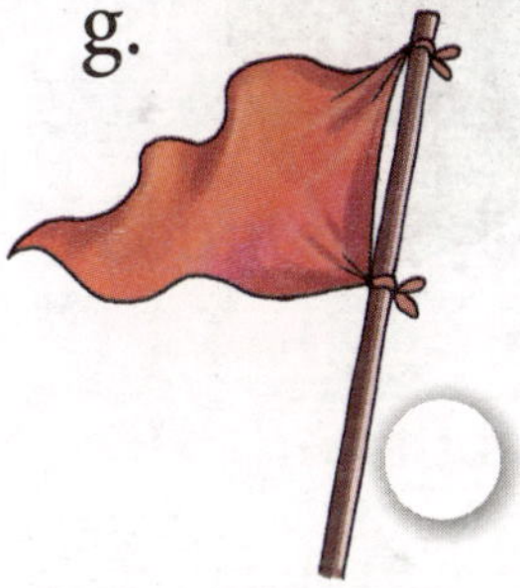

h.

i.

j.

C. Now look at these pictures. Can you name them?

1.

2.

3.

4.

5.

__ A __   __ E __ __   __ I __   __ O __   __ U __

COOL FACT A tongue twister is a sentence that has words that sound the same. So it is difficult to say quickly. A famous tongue twister is, she sells sea-shells on the seashore. Try to say it quickly and see what happens!

LOGICAL REASONING

21 Rough or Smooth

The things we touch can be rough or smooth.

A. *Look at the pictures below. They are rough or smooth to touch. In the boxes, write* R *for the things that are rough to touch and* S *for those that are smooth to touch.*

1.

2.

3.

4.

5.

6.

7.

8.

9.

10.

11.

B. *Bring to class a thing that is rough to touch and another that is smooth. Share them with your friends. Write their names below.*

Rough Thing	**Smooth Thing**
____________________	____________________
____________________	____________________

C. *Here are some more rough and smooth things. Find them and touch them and see for yourself!*

glazed paper

tree trunk

sandpaper

leaves

bricks

apple

sack

compact disc

Cool Activity

- Take coins of ₹1, ₹2 and ₹5.
- Cover each coin with a piece of white paper.
- Rub a pencil softly over the coin. Look at the paper.
- The design on the coin will show clearly on the paper!

What Comes First?

Which action would you do first? Write a or b in the given box.

1\.
a. 
Get up from bed. ☐

b. 
Have a glass of milk. ☐

2\.
a. 
Put on your socks and shoes. ☐

b. 
Wear your uniform. ☐

3\.
a. 
Brush your teeth. ☐

b. 
Have your breakfast. ☐

4\.
a. 
Comb your hair. ☐

b. 
Have a bath. ☐

5\.
a. 

Catch the school bus. ☐

b. 
Leave home for the bus stop. ☐

After School

Look at the pictures. Write a, b, c, d, e and f to arrange them in the order in which you do these actions when you come back home from school.

1.

2.

3.

4.

5.

6.

INDIA

22

Flowers in India

Flowers are beautiful things! They come in so many colours, they smell great and you can wear them, make your home pretty or give a lovely gift to your family and friends.

A. *Join the lines and pictures about these common Indian flowers.*

1 Lotus is the national flower of India	a. 	i. Strings of the flower make lovely garlands or decoration.
2 Marigold is a golden yellow or orange flower.	b. 	ii. It is used to make little garlands and flower-strings.
3 Jasmine is a small white flower with a lovely scent.	c. 	iii. But its stems have sharp thorns!
4 Rose has a lovely scent. It can have many colours like red, pink, yellow, white, and even black	d. 	iv. It grows in ponds and has floating leaves.

5 Flame of the Forest flowers are bright red-orange. They bloom from April to June.

e. 

v. It blooms at night and has a lovely scent.

6 Frangipani is a pretty white flower with five white petals with a little yellow near the middle.

f. 

vi. The ground beneath a tree in spring is covered in a bright red carpet of flowers!

7 Tuberose is a white flower with a long stem.

g. 

vii. It has a strong scent and large petals.

B. You may know the names of some of these flowers in your own language. Write them down and find out the others!

English name	Name in my language
Lotus	
Marigold	
Jasmine	
Rose	
Flame of the Forest	
Frangipani	
Tuberose	

COOL FACT In the state of Uttarakhand, about 17 km. from the town of Joshimath, amongst the Himalayan mountains lies the Valley of Flowers with about 500 kinds of flowers and many rare animals and birds.

SPORTS

23 Sporting Legends

What do you play? These Indians are great sportswomen. They have won many medals!

Fill in the blanks with the name of the sport.

1. Sania Mirza plays ______________ She plays with a tennis racquet and a tennis ball.

2. Geeta & Babita Phogat are sisters and ______________ champions. They wrestle on a mat.

3. Koneru Humpy plays ______________ She is a Grandmaster. She plays on a black and white board with 16 white and 16 black pieces.

4. PV Sindhu and Saina Nehwal play ____________ with a racquet and shuttlecock.

5. Karnam Malleswari is a ____________ champion. She can pick up very heavy dumbells!

6. Dipa Karmakar is a ____________ champion. She is very graceful and flexible.

COOL FACT

Tajamul Islam was born in 2008 in Kashmir. She is a kickboxer. She won a gold medal in Italy when she was just 8 years old!

Wrestling	Gymnastics
Tennis	Badminton
Chess	Weightlifting

Fun at the Zoo

Look at the zoo and say/show/do the following.

1. How many visitors can you see?
2. Name three animals that are eating fruits, vegetables or leaves.
3. Find and circle three snakes.
4. Name three heavy animals.
5. Circle three animals that roar.
6. Which are the three animals in water?
7. Say the names of three birds on the tree.
8. Circle three birds in the water.
9. What are four things that you should NOT do on a visit to a zoo? Circle them.
10. What are four fun things that you can do on a visit to a zoo? Circle them.

LOGICAL REASONING

24 More or Less

Look at each pair of pictures given below and answer the questions. Tick (✓) the right options.

1. Which is longer?

a. 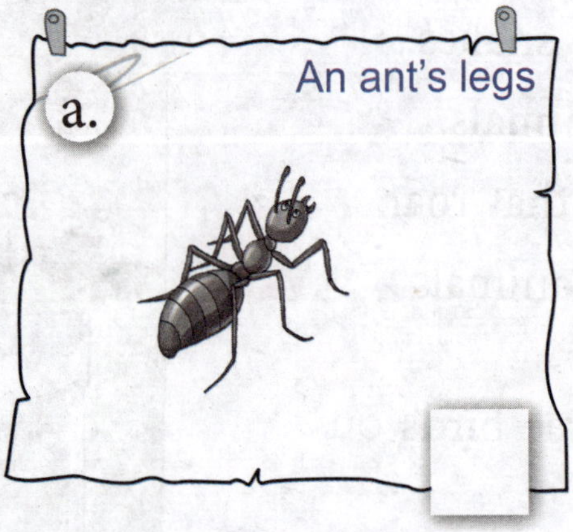

b. 

2. Which is higher?

a. 

b. 

3. Which is taller?

a. 

b. 

4. Which is heavier?

a. Your schoolbag

b. Two buckets full of water

5. Which is deeper?

a. The sea

b. A pond

6. Which is bigger?

a. A blue whale

b. An elephant

COOL FACT Mount Everest is the tallest mountain peak in the world and the highest point on Earth. It is 8,848 metres tall.
Cooler Fact: Its height is increasing every year.

SCIENCE

25

Know Your Computer

Tick (✓) the things that are part of a computer and cross (×) the things that are not.

1.  ☐

2.  ☐

3.  ☐

4.  ☐

5.  ☐

6.  ☐

7.  ☐

8. 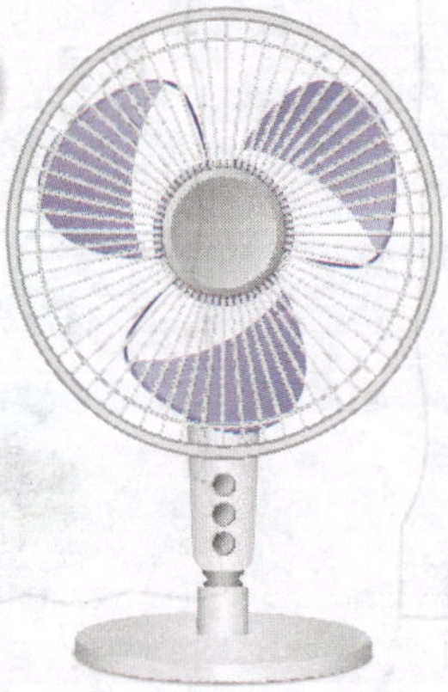 ☐

9. 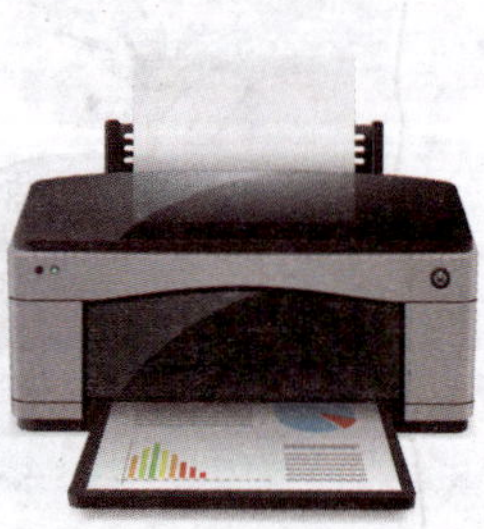 ☐

COOL FACT Charles Babbage is known as the 'Father of the Computer'.

26

SPORTS

Counting in Cricket

Cricket is a game of numbers. We count runs or team scores. Sometimes players break records too! But some numbers in cricket never change.

See if you can join cricket things with their numbers below.

1.	Number of players on the field from the fielding side	100
2.	Number of bails	0
3.	Number of runs in a century	3
4.	Number of runs scored in a maiden over	2
5.	Number of umpires on a field while a match is being played	4
6.	Number of balls in an over	5
7.	Number of wickets that make up a hat-trick	50
8.	Number of days in a test match	6
9.	Number of overs that one team can play in a One-Day International	11

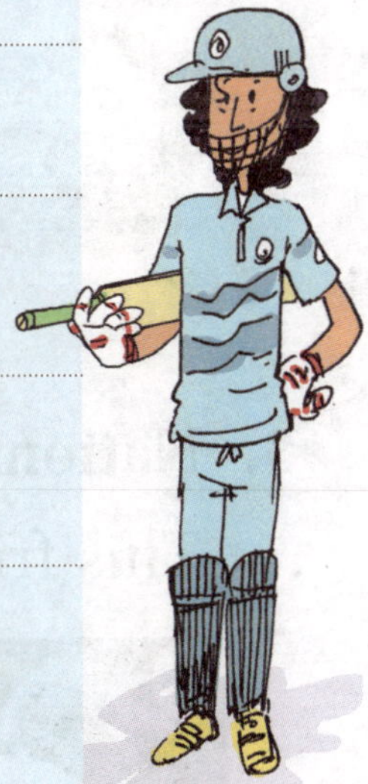

COOL FACT When a batsman gets out without scoring a run, it means that he has got a 'duck'.

27

National Symbols

Each of these rows tells you about a national symbol. Tick (✓) the right picture of the symbol in each row. Read the clues!

1. National Flag

The Indian National Flag has a blue wheel in the centre.

a.  ☐

b.  ☐

c.  ☐

2. National Animal

This animal is found in jungles all over India and it has stripes!

a.  ☐

b.  ☐

c.  ☐

3. National Aquatic Animal

This friendly, playful animal is found mainly in the river Ganga.

a.  ☐

b.  ☐

c.  ☐

4. **National Bird**

This multicoloured bird has beautiful tail feathers.

a

b

c

5. **National Fruit**

This golden fruit makes summer vacations sweeter!

a

b

c

6. **National Flower**

Usually pink or white, it has big round floating leaves!

a

b

c

7. **National Tree**

This huge and shady tree has lots of long, thick hanging roots.

a

b

c

SAFETY SCIENCE

28 Be Safe at Home

What should you do or should you not do at home? Match the pictures and sentences.

1.

Do not walk with a full glass of water or milk

a.

You can get a shock!

2.

Open and close windows/ doors with care

b.

It can spill!

3.

Do not stick your finger or a metal in a socket...

c.

Your finger can get jammed!

4.

Do not use metal dishes in a microwave oven

d.

It can poke someone in the eye!

5.

Open an umbrella very carefully

e.

You can get badly hurt or even end up in hospital

6.

Do not play rough games in the bath

f.

The oven will give out sparks and can catch fire!

Step Up!

To become a smart quizzer, we have learned how to find the odd one out. Now we will learn how to do it with real people, places, buildings and happenings.

Here is an example.

A. *Find the odd one from among these four famous people.*

a. 

Mahatma Gandhi

b. 

Pandit Nehru

c. 

Narendra Modi

d. 

Subhash Chandra Bose

Steps

To start with, let us see what is common to all of them.

1. All men
2. All Indians
3. All politicians

Now let us see what is different about them.

1. Two of them are Prime Ministers, one was the first Prime Minister, one is the Prime Minister right now, two were never Prime Ministers. So no odd one found.
2. Two Gujaratis, one Kashmiri and one Bengali. So no odd one found.
3. Three of them are not living now. Only one is living. That is Narendra Modi, so he is the odd one!

B. *Now, see if you can use the same steps to find answers to these quizzes and circle the odd one.*

1.

Qutb Minar

Eiffel Tower

Leaning Tower of Pisa

Great Wall of China

2.

Chennai

Mumbai

Gujarat

Kolkata

3.

Mahendra Singh Dhoni

Sushil Kumar

Suresh Raina

Virat Kohli

4.

Black Sea

Yellow River

Greenland

Red Sea

Shadow Play

A. *Match each thing with its right shadow. Be careful! Not all are correct.*

1. 

2. 

3. 

4. 

a. 

b. 

c. 

d. 

e. 

Can you tell the class how you chose the right shadow for each thing?

B. *Now have fun trying to make these shadows using your hands. Tell the class what these shadows look like.*

1. 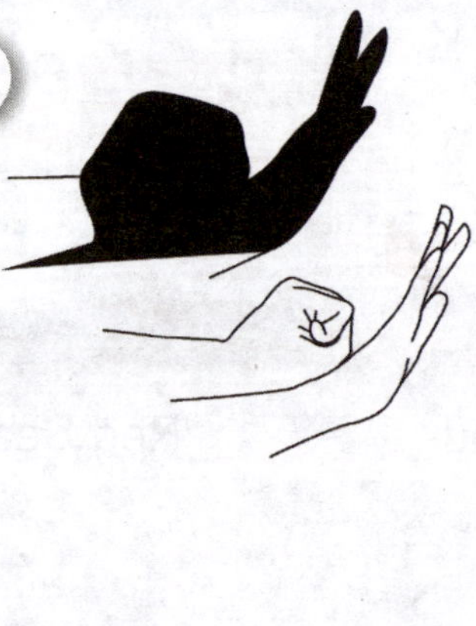

2. 

3. 

Keys

Page 12-13: smiley 1, 2, 4, 6, 7, 8, 10, 12, 13; sad face 3, 5, 9, 11, 14

Page 14: 1. circle; 2. triangle; 3. square; 4. rectangle; 5. oval; 6. star

Page 15: 1. f, lamb; 2. d, pup; 3. e, kid; 4. c, calf; 5. b, kitten; 6. a, foal

Page 16-17: 1. j; 2. d; 3. g; 4. e; 5. l; 6. i; 7. b; 8. l; 9. k; 10. k; 11. k; 12. k; 13. h; 14. k; 15. a; 16. f; 17. c; 18. m

Page 18: tick 3, 4, 5, 8, 9, 10; cross 1, 2, 6, 7

Page 19: A. watermelon: green outside, red inside; banana: yellow outside, white inside; pomegranate: light red outside, dark red inside; apple: red outside, white inside
B. watermelon - 2; apple - 3; orange - 2; banana - 4; papaya – 1

Page 20-21: A.

B. 1. four; 2. one; 3. four; 4. four

C.

Page 22: 1. a, b, c ; 2. a, b, d; 3. a, b, c; 4. a, c, d; 5. b, c, d

Page 23: 1. Spongebob Squarepants; 2. Doraemon; 3. Pikachu; 4. Teletubbies; 5. Thomas the Tank Engine Cool Quiz: Pingu

Page 24-25: summer green 1, 3, red 2, 4; monsoon green 3, red 1, 2, 4; winter green 1, 2, 3, red 4

Page 26-27: 1. S; 2. W; 3. W; 4. S; 5. S; 6. W; 7. W; 8. S; 9. W; 10. S

Page 28-29: green 2, 3, 5, 8, 10; red 1, 4, 6, 7, 9

Page 30-31: 1. d; 2. g; 3. e; 4. c; 5. h; 6. a; 7. f; 8. b

Page 32-33: pink a, b; red a, c; blue a, c; not white c; yellow a, c; green b, c; violet a, b; orange b, c

Page 34: A. 1. Diwali; 2. Janmashtami; 3. Eid; 4. Christmas; 5. Buddha Purnima; 6. Holi

Page 35: The 9 states that touch the sea are Gujarat, Maharashtra, Goa, Karnataka, Kerala, Tamil Nadu, Andhra Pradesh, Odisha and West Bengal

Page 36: A. 1. d; 2. f; 3. a; 4. b; 5. e; 6. c

Page 37: A. 1. chips; 2. milk; 3. chocolate; 4. cupcake; 5. Candy

Page 38-39: smiley 2, 3, 6; sad face: 1, 4, 5, 7, 9, 10

Page 42: 1. k+i; 2. a+g; 3. j+b; 4. c+h; 5. d+f; 6. l+e

Page 43: 1-a-ii; 2-b-iii; 3-c-i

Page 44-45: cows – moo-moo; sheep – baa-baa; horses – neigh-neigh; ducks – quack-quack; hens – cluck-cluck; dogs-bow-wow; cats – meow-meow

Page 46: 1. e; 2. c; 3. d; 4. a; 5. b

Page 47:

Page 48-49: A. 1. b; 2. a; 3. b; 4. b; 5. b; 6. a

Page 50-51: A. 1. b; 2. a; 3. c; 4. b; 5. d

Page 52-53: bedroom - a, h, k, n; bathroom - f, g, m, p; school bag - b, c, e, i; dining table - d, j, l, o

Page 54-55: 1. e; 2. d; 3. a; 4. f; 5. b; 6. c

Page 56-57: A. 1. mug; 2. jar; 3. ball; 4. bat; 5. cat; 6. dog; 7. man; 8. bag; 9. fan; 10. cap B. 1. b; 2. d; 3. i; 4. j; 5. h; 6. a; 7. f; 8. g; 9. c; 10. e C. 1. bag; 2. legs; 3. pin; 4. pot; 5. Sun

Page 58-59: A. R rough 2, 3, 6, 7, 10; S smooth 1, 4, 5, 8, 9, 11

Page 60-61: A. 1. a 1, b 2; 2. a 2, b 1; 3. a 1, b 2; 4. a 2, b 1; 5. a 2, b 1 B. 4. a; 5. b; 6. c; 1. d; 3. e; 2. f

Page 62-63: A. 1. c. iv; 2. a. i; 3. d. ii; 4. b. iii; 5. g. vi.; 6. f. vii; 7. e. v

Page 64-65: 1. Tennis; 2. Wrestling; 3. Chess; 4. Badminton; 5. Weightlifting; 6. Gymnastics

Page 66-67: 1. 10; 2. 4; 3. (in picture) snakes marked in red; 4. Giraffe, Deer, Monkey; 5. (in picture) marked in blue; 6. Crocodile, Rhinoceros, Hippopotamus; 7. hornbill, parrot, peacock; 8. (in picture) marked in pink; 9. (in picture) marked in green, 10. (in picture) marked in violet

Page 68-69: 1. b; 2. a; 3. b; 4. b; 5. a; 6. a

Page 70: Tick 2, 4, 5, 6, 7, 9; Cross 1, 3, 8

Page 71: 1. 11; 2. 4; 3. 100; 4. 0; 5. 2; 6. 6; 7. 3; 8. 5; 9. 50

Page 72-73: 1. a; 2. c; 3. c; 4. c; 5. b; 6. c; 7. b

Page 74-75: 1. b; 2. c; 3. a; 4. f; 5. d; 6. e

Page 76-77: B. 1. d; 2. c; 3. b; 4. c

Page 78: A. 1. c; 2. b; 3. e; 4. a B. 1. snail; 2. rabbit; 3. Elephant